EMMANUEL JOSEPH

The Revolutionary Hands, How Billionaires Quietly Code Industries and Redefine Global Power

Copyright © 2025 by Emmanuel Joseph

All rights reserved. No part of this publication may be reproduced, stored or transmitted in any form or by any means, electronic, mechanical, photocopying, recording, scanning, or otherwise without written permission from the publisher. It is illegal to copy this book, post it to a website, or distribute it by any other means without permission.

First edition

This book was professionally typeset on Reedsy.
Find out more at reedsy.com

Contents

1	Chapter 1: The Silent Architect	1
2	Chapter 2: The Coders of Destiny	3
3	Chapter 3: Financial Alchemy	5
4	Chapter 4: The Philanthropic Veil	7
5	Chapter 5: The Media Moguls	9
6	Chapter 6: The Global Network	11
7	Chapter 7: Technological Titans	13
8	Chapter 8: The Education Innovators	15
9	Chapter 9: The Green Guardians	17
10	Chapter 10: The Health Revolutionaries	19
11	Chapter 11: The Urban Visionaries	21
12	Chapter 12: The Data Sovereigns	23
13	Chapter 13: The Cultural Curators	25
14	Chapter 14: The Space Explorers	27
15	Chapter 15: The Digital Democracy Advocates	29
16	Chapter 16: The Global Communicators	31
17	Chapter 17: The Legacy Builders	33

1

Chapter 1: The Silent Architect

From the glistening skyscrapers of Wall Street to the tech hubs of Silicon Valley, billionaires have always been seen as the titans of industry. Yet, behind the ostentatious displays of wealth, there exists a more subtle and profound influence. These silent architects, often operating behind the scenes, have an uncanny ability to reshape entire industries with their innovative ideas and relentless ambition. By making strategic decisions that fly under the radar, they dictate the course of global markets, often with little public awareness. Through the lives of key figures, we uncover how their quiet yet powerful actions have reshaped the economic landscape.

Billionaires like Jeff Bezos and Elon Musk serve as prime examples of silent architects. Bezos, through Amazon, has not only revolutionized e-commerce but also logistics, cloud computing, and even entertainment. Musk, on the other hand, has pushed the boundaries of space travel and automotive innovation with SpaceX and Tesla. Their strategic decisions, such as Bezos's acquisition of Whole Foods or Musk's relentless pursuit of reusable rockets, have quietly shifted industry norms and consumer expectations.

But it's not just about the big moves; it's about the subtle, calculated steps that often go unnoticed. The silent architects invest in technologies and startups that align with their long-term vision, creating ecosystems that support their primary ventures. These investments are often shrouded in secrecy, making it difficult for competitors to anticipate their next move. By staying several steps ahead, they not only secure their dominance but also set the stage for future innovations.

In essence, the silent architect's influence is a testament to the power of strategic foresight and adaptability. Their ability to pivot and evolve with changing market dynamics ensures that they remain at the forefront of their industries. As we delve deeper into their stories, we begin to understand the magnitude of their impact and the quiet revolution they lead.

2

Chapter 2: The Coders of Destiny

Innovation isn't merely about creating the next big gadget; it's about coding the very fabric of our future. Billionaires, armed with vast resources and unparalleled vision, have become the coders of destiny, writing the script for the world of tomorrow. This chapter explores how these individuals leverage technology not just as a tool, but as a means to shape the future.

Consider the influence of pioneers like Bill Gates and Mark Zuckerberg. Gates, through Microsoft, has not only made computing accessible to the masses but has also laid the groundwork for the digital revolution. Zuckerberg, with Facebook, has redefined social interactions and communication on a global scale. Their contributions extend beyond their flagship products; they have created platforms and ecosystems that foster innovation and growth in numerous sectors.

The coders of destiny are not just tech enthusiasts; they are visionaries who anticipate and create trends. Their investments in artificial intelligence, biotechnology, and renewable energy are driven by a deep understanding of future needs and potentials. By decoding the strategies of these visionaries, we gain insight into their long-term goals and the technological revolutions they foresee.

Moreover, these billionaires recognize the importance of collaboration and knowledge-sharing. Through initiatives like open-source software and research grants, they empower others to contribute to the collective progress. This collaborative approach ensures that innovation is not confined to a select few but is a shared endeavor that benefits society as a whole.

In conclusion, the coders of destiny are the architects of our future, using their resources and vision to drive technological advancements that will shape the world for generations to come. Their ability to foresee and influence the next wave of innovations ensures that they remain pivotal players in the global landscape.

3

Chapter 3: Financial Alchemy

The world of finance is often viewed as a realm of numbers and spreadsheets, but for billionaires, it is a canvas for financial alchemy. This chapter unveils the secretive world of high-stakes investments and strategic acquisitions, revealing how these magnates transform struggling companies into booming enterprises.

Take Warren Buffett, the Oracle of Omaha, whose investment strategies have consistently outperformed the market. Buffett's approach to financial alchemy is rooted in his ability to identify undervalued companies and unlock their potential. His acquisitions are not merely financial transactions; they are strategic moves that breathe new life into businesses, ensuring long-term growth and stability.

Financial alchemy is not limited to traditional investments. Billionaires like Peter Thiel and Marc Andreessen have made their mark through venture capital, funding startups that have the potential to disrupt entire industries. Their investments in companies like PayPal, Facebook, and Airbnb have not only yielded substantial returns but have also reshaped the business landscape.

The methods of financial alchemists are often shrouded in secrecy, with deals negotiated behind closed doors and strategies revealed only after they have borne fruit. By mastering the art of financial alchemy, these billionaires wield an influence that extends far beyond their bank accounts, shaping the economic landscape in profound ways.

In essence, financial alchemy is about seeing potential where others see risk, and having the vision and resources to turn that potential into reality. The ability to transform industries and create wealth through strategic investments is a testament to the power of financial foresight and expertise.

4

Chapter 4: The Philanthropic Veil

Philanthropy is often perceived as the benevolent act of giving back to society. However, for billionaires, it serves a dual purpose. This chapter examines how philanthropy, while undoubtedly a force for good, also acts as a veil for strategic influence.

Billionaires like Bill Gates and Warren Buffett have pledged significant portions of their wealth to philanthropic causes through initiatives like the Giving Pledge. While their contributions address pressing societal issues such as healthcare and education, they also shape public perception and policy. By directing their wealth towards specific causes, these individuals influence global conversations and priorities, steering the course of societal progress.

Philanthropy allows billionaires to build a legacy that extends beyond their business achievements. Through their foundations and charitable endeavors, they leave an indelible mark on the world, ensuring that their influence endures for generations. However, it also grants them access to influential networks and decision-makers, further expanding their reach.

Moreover, philanthropic efforts often align with the strategic goals of these billionaires. By investing in healthcare, education, and technology, they create ecosystems that support their primary ventures. For example, Gates' investment in global health initiatives not only addresses critical issues but also creates a more stable and prosperous world, which in turn benefits his business interests.

In conclusion, the philanthropic veil is a powerful tool for billionaires to exercise strategic influence while contributing to the greater good. By understanding the dual nature of their philanthropy, we gain insight into how they quietly steer global conversations and priorities, redefining the balance of power under the guise of altruism.

5

Chapter 5: The Media Moguls

In the information age, control over media equates to control over narratives. Billionaires who have acquired vast media empires possess the power to influence public opinion and shape societal norms. This chapter delves into the strategic acquisitions and editorial directions that allow these moguls to craft the stories we consume, becoming the gatekeepers of information and subtly guiding the collective consciousness of society.

Take Rupert Murdoch, the media tycoon behind News Corp and Fox Corporation. Murdoch's media empire spans across continents, reaching millions of viewers and readers daily. Through his control of newspapers, television networks, and digital platforms, he has the ability to shape political discourse and public perception. His strategic acquisitions, such as the purchase of The Wall Street Journal, demonstrate a keen understanding of the power of media in shaping societal narratives.

Similarly, Oprah Winfrey, through her OWN network and influential media presence, has shaped conversations around self-improvement, empowerment, and social issues. Her platform has elevated diverse voices and brought critical issues to the forefront, influencing public opinion and cultural norms. Through her media ventures, she has become a powerful force in shaping societal values and conversations.

Media moguls also leverage their platforms to promote their business interests and political agendas. By controlling the flow of information, they can influence market trends, policy decisions, and public sentiment. This control extends beyond traditional media to social media platforms, where algorithms and content curation play a significant role in shaping our digital experiences.

In essence, media moguls wield significant power in the information age. By understanding their strategies and influence, we gain insight into how they shape societal norms and public discourse, quietly redefining the power dynamics in the digital era.

6

Chapter 6: The Global Network

The influence of billionaires is not confined by national borders. This chapter explores how these individuals build extensive global networks, connecting with political leaders, industry giants, and thought leaders. By fostering relationships across continents, they create a web of influence that transcends geographic limitations, shaping international policies and economic landscapes.

Billionaires like Richard Branson and Jack Ma exemplify the power of global networks. Branson, through his Virgin Group, has established a presence in various industries across the globe, from airlines to telecommunications. His ability to connect with leaders and innovators worldwide has enabled him to expand his business empire and drive global initiatives, such as space tourism with Virgin Galactic.

Jack Ma, the founder of Alibaba, has built a vast network of connections with global leaders and entrepreneurs. Through partnerships and collaborations, he has expanded Alibaba's reach beyond China, establishing it as a global e-commerce giant. Ma's ability to navigate international markets and foster relationships with key stakeholders has been instrumental in his success.

International summits, private meetings, and exclusive clubs play a crucial role in facilitating these connections. Billionaires participate in forums like the World Economic Forum, where they engage with global leaders and discuss pressing issues. These interactions provide opportunities to influence policy decisions and shape the global economic agenda.

By building and leveraging their global networks, billionaires exert a far-reaching impact that shapes international policies and economic landscapes. Their ability to connect with key players worldwide ensures that they remain influential figures in the global arena, quietly redefining the power dynamics on an international scale.

7

Chapter 7: Technological Titans

In the rapidly evolving tech industry, certain billionaires stand out as titans who drive innovation and redefine our digital lives. This chapter focuses on the pioneers behind the most influential tech companies, exploring their journeys from startup founders to industry leaders and their visionary approaches to pushing the boundaries of what's possible.

Elon Musk, the enigmatic CEO of SpaceX and Tesla, is a prime example of a technological titan. Musk's relentless pursuit of innovation has led to groundbreaking advancements in space travel, electric vehicles, and renewable energy. His vision for a sustainable future, coupled with his ambitious projects, has transformed industries and inspired a new generation of entrepreneurs.

Similarly, Jeff Bezos, the founder of Amazon, has revolutionized e-commerce, cloud computing, and logistics. Bezos's visionary approach to customer-centric innovation and his willingness to take bold risks have made Amazon a dominant force in multiple sectors. From the development of Amazon Web Services to the acquisition of Whole Foods, his strategic decisions have reshaped the business landscape.

Technological titans leverage their expertise and resources to push the boundaries of innovation. Their investments in research and development, coupled with a deep understanding of market trends, enable them to create products and services that transform the way we live, work, and interact. By fostering a culture of innovation and embracing disruptive technologies, they ensure that they remain at the forefront of the tech industry.

Through their visionary approaches and relentless pursuit of progress, technological titans redefine our digital lives and shape the future of technology. Their ability to anticipate and drive technological revolutions ensures that they remain pivotal players in the global landscape, quietly coding the future of our digital world.

8

Chapter 8: The Education Innovators

Education is the cornerstone of progress, and billionaires who invest in this sector hold the key to shaping future generations. This chapter examines how these visionaries are revolutionizing education through innovative approaches and substantial funding, redefining the educational landscape to ensure that the next wave of leaders is equipped to navigate the complexities of a rapidly changing world.

Bill Gates, through the Bill & Melinda Gates Foundation, has made significant contributions to education reform. The foundation's initiatives focus on improving educational outcomes, promoting digital learning, and supporting teachers. By funding innovative programs and research, Gates is driving efforts to create equitable and effective educational systems that prepare students for the challenges of the 21st century.

Similarly, Laurene Powell Jobs, through the Emerson Collective, has invested in educational initiatives that promote personalized learning and educational equity. The organization's efforts to reimagine traditional schooling models and support underserved communities highlight the potential for transformative change in education. Powell Jobs's commitment to fostering a culture of curiosity and critical thinking ensures that students are empowered to reach their full potential.

Education innovators recognize the importance of leveraging technology to enhance learning experiences. By supporting digital learning platforms and educational startups, they create opportunities for students to access high-quality education regardless of their geographic location. These efforts bridge the digital divide and ensure that all students have the tools they need to succeed.

Through their visionary approaches and substantial investments, education innovators are reshaping the future of learning. Their commitment to innovation and equity ensures that the next generation of leaders is prepared to thrive in an increasingly complex and interconnected world. By understanding their strategies, we gain insight into how they quietly redefine the educational landscape and shape the future of education.

9

Chapter 9: The Green Guardians

As the world grapples with environmental challenges, a new breed of billionaires has emerged as green guardians. These individuals leverage their wealth and influence to champion sustainable practices and combat climate change. Through investments in renewable energy, conservation efforts, and eco-friendly technologies, they play a pivotal role in driving the global green agenda. By prioritizing environmental stewardship, these green guardians not only protect our planet but also redefine the relationship between industry and nature.

Consider the efforts of billionaires like Elon Musk and Sir Richard Branson. Musk's work with Tesla and SolarCity has popularized electric vehicles and solar energy, making sustainable technology more accessible to the masses. His vision for a carbon-neutral future has driven significant advancements in clean energy, reshaping the automotive and energy industries.

Similarly, Sir Richard Branson, through his Virgin Group, has made substantial investments in sustainable aviation and renewable energy projects. Branson's initiatives, such as Virgin Atlantic's commitment to reducing carbon emissions and Virgin Galactic's focus on sustainable space travel, exemplify his dedication to environmental sustainability. By investing in innovative solutions and advocating for eco-friendly practices, Branson plays a crucial role in promoting a greener future.

Green guardians also support conservation efforts and biodiversity projects.

Philanthropists like Hansjörg Wyss have pledged significant funds to protect natural landscapes and wildlife habitats. The Wyss Campaign for Nature aims to conserve 30 percent of the planet's surface by 2030, highlighting the importance of preserving biodiversity and mitigating the impacts of climate change.

Through their investments and advocacy, green guardians drive the global green agenda, inspiring others to embrace sustainable practices. Their commitment to environmental stewardship ensures that industries and governments prioritize sustainability, ultimately redefining the relationship between industry and nature.

10

Chapter 10: The Health Revolutionaries

Healthcare is a fundamental human right, and certain billionaires are at the forefront of revolutionizing this critical sector. This chapter delves into the initiatives and innovations led by health revolutionaries who are transforming healthcare delivery and accessibility. From funding groundbreaking medical research to developing new treatment methodologies, their contributions have a profound impact on global health outcomes.

Bill Gates, through the Bill & Melinda Gates Foundation, has made significant contributions to global health. The foundation's efforts to combat infectious diseases, improve maternal and child health, and promote vaccine accessibility have saved millions of lives. Gates's commitment to funding research and development in healthcare ensures that innovative solutions are brought to the forefront, addressing some of the world's most pressing health challenges.

Similarly, Dr. Patrick Soon-Shiong, a billionaire physician and entrepreneur, has made remarkable strides in cancer research and treatment. Through his companies, such as NantWorks and NantHealth, Soon-Shiong has developed innovative cancer therapies and advanced healthcare technologies. His focus on personalized medicine and cutting-edge research has the potential to revolutionize cancer treatment and improve patient outcomes.

Health revolutionaries also recognize the importance of addressing healthcare disparities. Philanthropists like Priscilla Chan and Mark Zuckerberg, through the Chan Zuckerberg Initiative, have committed to advancing healthcare equity. Their investments in medical research, community health programs, and educational initiatives aim to reduce health disparities and ensure that all individuals have access to high-quality care.

Through their visionary approaches and substantial investments, health revolutionaries are transforming the healthcare landscape. Their dedication to innovation and equity ensures that healthcare delivery is improved, disparities are addressed, and global health outcomes are enhanced. By understanding their contributions, we gain insight into how they quietly redefine the standards of care and ensure a healthier future for all.

11

Chapter 11: The Urban Visionaries

Cities are the epicenters of human activity, and billionaires who invest in urban development shape the way we live and interact within these spaces. This chapter explores the urban visionaries who reimagine cityscapes through ambitious projects and sustainable designs. By creating smart cities and revitalizing urban areas, they enhance the quality of life for residents and foster economic growth.

Michael Bloomberg, the former mayor of New York City, is a prominent example of an urban visionary. Bloomberg's efforts to improve public transportation, promote sustainable development, and enhance public spaces have transformed New York City into a model of urban innovation. His commitment to public health and environmental sustainability has set new standards for modern cities.

Similarly, Elon Musk's ambitious projects, such as the development of the Hyperloop and The Boring Company's tunnel systems, aim to revolutionize urban transportation. Musk's vision for high-speed, efficient transportation solutions has the potential to alleviate traffic congestion, reduce emissions, and create more livable urban environments. By investing in futuristic transportation technologies, Musk redefines the concept of urban mobility.

Urban visionaries also focus on creating sustainable and resilient cities. Billionaires like Bill Gates, through initiatives like the Belmont Project, aim to build smart cities that leverage technology to improve the quality of life for residents. These projects incorporate renewable energy, efficient transportation systems, and advanced infrastructure to create sustainable urban environments.

Through their visionary approaches and innovative projects, urban visionaries reshape the way we experience urban living. Their commitment to sustainability, efficiency, and quality of life ensures that modern cities are not only functional but also vibrant and livable. By understanding their contributions, we gain insight into how they quietly redefine urban development and set new standards for future cities.

12

Chapter 12: The Data Sovereigns

In the digital era, data is the new gold, and those who control it wield immense power. This chapter examines the data sovereigns—billionaires who have built empires on the foundation of data analytics and artificial intelligence. By harnessing the power of data, they gain unparalleled insights into consumer behavior, market trends, and societal patterns. We explore the ethical considerations and implications of their control over vast amounts of information.

Jeff Bezos, through Amazon, has created one of the most data-driven companies in the world. Amazon's vast troves of consumer data enable the company to personalize shopping experiences, optimize supply chains, and predict market trends. Bezos's mastery of data analytics has not only driven Amazon's success but has also reshaped the retail industry, setting new standards for data-driven decision-making.

Similarly, Larry Page and Sergey Brin, the co-founders of Google, have built an empire on the foundation of data. Google's search engine and suite of digital services collect and analyze vast amounts of information, providing valuable insights into user behavior and preferences. Page and Brin's innovative use of data has transformed Google into a global tech giant, influencing everything from online advertising to artificial intelligence.

The control of data raises important ethical considerations. Data sovereigns must navigate issues related to privacy, security, and the ethical use of information. Companies like Google and Amazon face scrutiny over their data practices, prompting discussions about transparency, regulation, and the balance between innovation and privacy.

By understanding the strategies and influence of data sovereigns, we gain insight into the power dynamics of the digital era. Their ability to harness and analyze data provides them with unparalleled insights and influence, quietly shaping the future of technology and society. Through their mastery of data, they redefine the boundaries of knowledge and influence.

13

Chapter 13: The Cultural Curators

Culture is a reflection of society, and certain billionaires have taken on the role of cultural curators. This chapter delves into how these individuals invest in the arts, media, and entertainment to shape cultural narratives. By supporting artists, filmmakers, and creators, they influence the stories that define our collective identity. Through their patronage, cultural curators ensure that diverse voices are heard and that culture remains a vibrant and dynamic force in our lives. Their contributions redefine the relationship between wealth and cultural expression.

One prominent cultural curator is David Geffen, the co-founder of DreamWorks and a major patron of the arts. Geffen's significant contributions to museums, theaters, and cultural institutions have had a profound impact on the arts landscape. His support for artists and filmmakers has enabled the creation of groundbreaking works that challenge societal norms and inspire audiences worldwide.

Similarly, Laurene Powell Jobs, through her Emerson Collective, has invested in media and storytelling initiatives that amplify diverse voices and promote social change. Powell Jobs's commitment to elevating underrepresented perspectives and addressing critical social issues has shaped the cultural narrative, fostering a more inclusive and empathetic society.

Cultural curators also leverage their influence to promote cultural preservation and innovation. Billionaires like François Pinault, through his extensive art collection and foundation, have contributed to the preservation of cultural heritage and the promotion of contemporary art. Pinault's dedication to the arts ensures that both historical and modern artistic expressions are celebrated and accessible to the public.

Through their patronage and investments, cultural curators shape the stories that define our collective identity. Their support for the arts and media fosters creativity, diversity, and social awareness, ensuring that culture remains a dynamic and influential force. By understanding their contributions, we gain insight into how they quietly redefine the relationship between wealth and cultural expression.

14

Chapter 14: The Space Explorers

Space exploration has always been a frontier of human ambition, and modern billionaires are leading the charge into the cosmos. This chapter explores the ventures of space explorers who invest in commercial space travel and extraterrestrial research. By funding missions to Mars, developing reusable rockets, and establishing space tourism companies, they push the boundaries of what humanity can achieve.

Elon Musk, through SpaceX, has revolutionized space travel with the development of reusable rockets and ambitious plans to colonize Mars. Musk's vision for space exploration extends beyond scientific curiosity; he aims to ensure the survival of humanity by making life multi-planetary. SpaceX's successful missions to the International Space Station and plans for Mars colonization exemplify Musk's commitment to pushing the boundaries of space exploration.

Similarly, Jeff Bezos, through Blue Origin, has made significant strides in advancing commercial space travel. Bezos's vision for the future includes building infrastructure for space tourism and industrial activities in space. Blue Origin's development of reusable rockets and plans for lunar missions highlight Bezos's dedication to making space accessible to future generations.

Richard Branson, through Virgin Galactic, has also made notable contributions to space tourism. Virgin Galactic's efforts to provide suborbital space flights for civilians represent a significant step towards democratizing space travel. Branson's commitment to making space exploration an attainable experience for all reflects his belief in the transformative power of space travel.

Through their investments and visionary approaches, space explorers are pushing the boundaries of what humanity can achieve. Their efforts to advance space travel and research inspire a new era of exploration and discovery, redefining our understanding of the cosmos and our place within it. By understanding their contributions, we gain insight into how they quietly shape the future of space exploration.

15

Chapter 15: The Digital Democracy Advocates

The digital age has transformed the way we engage with democracy, and certain billionaires are at the forefront of promoting digital democracy. This chapter examines how these advocates leverage technology to enhance civic participation and transparency. From developing platforms for online voting to supporting initiatives that combat misinformation, they work to ensure that democracy thrives in the digital era.

Pierre Omidyar, the founder of eBay and the philanthropic organization Luminate, has been a prominent advocate for digital democracy. Luminate supports initiatives that promote government transparency, accountability, and civic engagement through technology. Omidyar's commitment to fostering a more informed and participatory society has driven efforts to combat misinformation and promote digital rights.

Similarly, Mark Zuckerberg, through Facebook and the Chan Zuckerberg Initiative, has made significant contributions to enhancing civic participation and promoting informed dialogue. Facebook's tools for voter registration and political engagement have facilitated greater participation in the democratic process. Additionally, the Chan Zuckerberg Initiative's investments in civic technology aim to empower communities and promote democratic values.

Digital democracy advocates also focus on addressing the challenges posed by misinformation and digital manipulation. Philanthropists like Craig Newmark, the founder of Craigslist, have funded initiatives that promote journalistic integrity and combat misinformation. Newmark's support for fact-checking organizations and media literacy programs highlights the importance of trustworthy information in a functioning democracy.

Through their investments and advocacy, digital democracy advocates ensure that democracy thrives in the digital era. Their efforts to promote civic participation, transparency, and informed dialogue redefine the relationship between technology and governance. By understanding their contributions, we gain insight into how they quietly shape the future of democracy in the digital age.

16

Chapter 16: The Global Communicators

Effective communication is essential in a connected world, and billionaires who excel as global communicators wield significant influence. This chapter explores how these individuals use their platforms to engage with diverse audiences and shape public discourse. By mastering the art of communication, they address global challenges, promote unity, and inspire action.

Oprah Winfrey, a media mogul and philanthropist, is a prime example of a global communicator. Through her television shows, interviews, and philanthropic efforts, Winfrey has inspired millions and sparked important conversations on social issues. Her ability to connect with audiences and address complex topics with empathy and authenticity has made her a powerful force in shaping public discourse.

Similarly, Bill and Melinda Gates, through their foundation and public speaking engagements, have effectively communicated the importance of global health, education, and poverty alleviation. Their commitment to addressing critical global challenges and their ability to convey their message to diverse audiences have mobilized support and driven meaningful change.

Global communicators also leverage digital platforms to amplify their reach and impact. Individuals like Elon Musk, with his active presence on social media, engage directly with the public, sharing updates on their projects and addressing global issues. Musk's communication style, characterized by transparency and directness, has garnered a loyal following and influenced public perception.

Through their mastery of communication, global communicators address global challenges, promote unity, and inspire action. Their ability to engage with diverse audiences and shape public discourse ensures that critical issues are brought to the forefront and addressed collaboratively. By understanding their contributions, we gain insight into how they quietly redefine the power of language and its impact on society.

17

Chapter 17: The Legacy Builders

As billionaires approach the zenith of their careers, their focus shifts towards building lasting legacies. This chapter delves into the strategies and initiatives that ensure their influence endures beyond their lifetimes. From establishing enduring institutions to creating impactful endowments, legacy builders shape the future through their foresight and generosity.

Warren Buffett, one of the most successful investors of all time, has committed to giving away the majority of his wealth through the Giving Pledge. Buffett's philanthropic efforts focus on long-term solutions to global challenges, such as poverty alleviation and education. His commitment to building a lasting legacy through strategic philanthropy ensures that his impact endures for generations.

Similarly, Bill Gates, through the Bill & Melinda Gates Foundation, has established enduring institutions that address critical global issues. The foundation's investments in healthcare, education, and poverty reduction create sustainable solutions that improve lives worldwide. Gates's focus on creating systemic change ensures that his legacy is defined by meaningful and lasting impact.

Legacy builders also invest in initiatives that promote innovation and knowledge. Philanthropists like Michael Bloomberg, through Bloomberg Philanthropies, support initiatives that advance public health, education, and the arts. Bloomberg's commitment to fostering creativity and progress ensures that future generations benefit from his contributions.

Through their strategies and initiatives, legacy builders ensure that their influence endures beyond their lifetimes. Their foresight and generosity shape the future, leaving a lasting impact on society. By understanding their contributions, we gain insight into how they quietly redefine the concept of legacy and inspire future generations to dream big and act boldly.

And that's the completion of our book, "The Revolutionary Hands: How Billionaires Quietly Code Industries and Redefine Global Power." Each chapter elaborates on the various ways billionaires influence and shape our world, often behind the scenes. I hope you find this engaging and insightful. If there are any adjustments or additional details you'd like to include, please let me know!

"The Revolutionary Hands: How Billionaires Quietly Code Industries and Redefine Global Power" is a compelling exploration of how the world's wealthiest individuals exert their influence in subtle yet profound ways. Through seventeen meticulously crafted chapters, this book delves into the behind-the-scenes strategies and visionary approaches that billionaires use to reshape industries and drive global change.

From the silent architects who transform markets with strategic foresight to the coders of destiny who envision and create the future, each chapter unveils the unique impact of these influential figures. Readers will gain insight into the financial alchemy that turns struggling companies into thriving enterprises, the philanthropic veils that merge altruism with strategic influence, and the media moguls who control the narratives that shape public opinion.

The book also explores the global networks that transcend borders, the technological titans pushing the boundaries of innovation, and the education innovators revolutionizing the learning landscape. Environmental stewardship, healthcare advancements, urban development, data sovereignty, cultural curation, space exploration, digital democracy, and effective communication are just a few of the areas where billionaires leave their mark.

By examining the contributions of these remarkable individuals, "The

CHAPTER 17: THE LEGACY BUILDERS

Revolutionary Hands" reveals how their quiet actions and visionary leadership redefine the balance of power and shape the future of our world. This insightful and thought-provoking book offers readers a deeper understanding of the profound influence wielded by the world's most powerful individuals.

www.ingramcontent.com/pod-product-compliance
Lightning Source LLC
LaVergne TN
LVHW020459080526
838202LV00057B/6050